Children's Champion

MARIAN WRIGHT EDELMAN

by Joann J. Burch

A Gateway Biography
The Millbrook Press
Brookfield, Connecticut

For Berkeley, Robert, and Barry

Cover photo courtesy of Eddie Adams, Sygma
Background cover photo courtesy of Superstock

Photos courtesy of AP/Wide World: pp. 4, 18, 40 (bottom);
Children's Defense Fund: pp. 9, 15 (top), 36; Schomburg
Center for Research in Black Culture, New York Public
Library: pp. 11, 15 (bottom), 23, 26; Matt Heron, Black
Star: p. 21 (top); UPI/Bettmann: pp. 21 (bottom), 30, 33;
Peggy Harrison, CDF: p. 39; Najlah Feanny, Saba: p. 40
(top); Jonathan Levine: p. 43.

Library of Congress Cataloging-in-Publication Data
Burch, Joann Johansen.
Marian Wright Edelman, children's champion
by Joann J. Burch.
p.   cm.—(A Gateway biography)
Includes bibliographical references and index.
Summary: Tells the life story of the founder of the
Children's Defense Fund. It traces her life from her
modest beginnings in the rural, segregated South to her
rise to prominence as the most respected advocate
of children's rights in the United States.
ISBN 1-56294-457-6 (lib. bdg.)   ISBN 1-56294-742-7 (pbk.)
1. Edelman, Marian Wright—Juvenile literature.   2. Afro-
Americans—Biography—Juvenile literature.   3. Social
reformers—United States—Biography—Juvenile literature.
4. Children's rights—United States—History—20th century
—Juvenile literature.   5. Civil rights workers—United
States—Biography—Juvenile literature.   [1. Edelman,
Marian Wright.   2. Reformers.   3. Afro-Americans—
Biography.   4. Children's rights.]   I. Title.   II. Series.
E185.97.E33B86   1994   973'.0496073'02—dc20
[B]   94-2260   CIP   AC

Published by The Millbrook Press
2 Old New Milford Road
Brookfield, Connecticut 06804

Marian Wright Edelman

Marian Wright visited poor people in the Mississippi Delta with Robert Kennedy and other U.S. senators. Wright wanted the senators to see how hard life was for poor Americans, like the woman in this photo.

Marian *Wright* stood tall and straight before the four U.S. senators. The senators had come to Jackson, Mississippi, to learn more about poverty. The year was 1967, and some areas of Mississippi ranked among the poorest in the nation. Twenty-seven-year-old Wright was a lawyer dedicated to helping Mississippi's needy, especially its children.

"People are starving," Wright told the senators. "I wish the senators would have a chance to go around and just look at the empty cupboards . . . and the number of people who are going around begging just to feed their children."

Senators Robert Kennedy and Joseph Clark granted Wright's wish. They joined her on a tour of Mississippi's poorest areas. They visited homes in the Delta, the western part of the state where people farmed cotton and beans. Many of the houses were nothing more than shacks with dirt floors and walls papered with newspapers. Very few had heat, electricity, or running water.

A little boy stood outside one windowless shack. He led Wright and the senators inside. The place was dark and smelled of mildew, sickness, and urine. A small stove sat in one corner. Across the room, a bed was propped up by bricks to keep it from falling over. A baby sat on the floor, his stomach swollen from malnutrition. Open sores covered his body.

Kennedy picked up the baby, rubbing his stomach and soothing him. When the child did not react, Kennedy tried tickling him, something most children enjoy. This child, however, stared straight ahead, as if he were in a trance. Angry tears ran down Kennedy's cheeks. "I'm going back to Washington to do something about this," he declared.

Marian Wright had helped Senator Kennedy understand the depth of the suffering of poor people and their children. It was not the first time that she had made ending their plight the responsibility of politicians and others, nor would it be the last. This was why she became known as the children's champion.

Marian Wright was born in the rural town of Bennettsville, South Carolina, on June 6, 1939. Her family name was Wright. She added Edelman to her name when she married Peter Edelman in 1968. Marian was the youngest of five children in her close-knit family. Her father, Arthur Wright, was minister of the Shiloh Baptist Church. Her mother, Maggie Wright, played the church organ and helped raise money to support the church and its many projects.

Although the family never had much money, Marian felt loved and valued. She recalled, "The world outside said we were poor black kids who weren't worth much, but the family said that wasn't so, and the church said it wasn't so." In the 1940s, some southern whites thought poor black children were second-class citizens who would never amount to anything.

Arthur and Maggie Wright expected their children to amount to something. That meant being helpful to others, getting good grades in school, and reading. All of the Wright children attended the nightly study hour around the family dinner table. From 6:30 to 7:30 they did homework. If they had no assignments, their father would say, "Well, assign yourself." Marian's brother Harry said, "It was just read, read, read."

Besides reading, Marian and her siblings were expected to do chores. The boys knew how to make beds and clean house as well as the girls, and at night they helped wash the dishes. The girls learned how to wax cars and change tires just as the boys did. Marian played with cars and trains far more than with dolls.

She and her brothers and sister also helped out in their community. When Marian was nine years old, she went with an older brother to treat the sores that a sick neighbor had gotten from being bedridden. She learned how much even the smallest hands could mean to a sick person. Working for the community was as much a part of her family's existence as eating and sleeping and church.

Arthur Wright taught by example how to make the community a better place to live. Bennettsville was a typical segregated southern town during the time Marian was growing up. "Segregated" means that blacks and whites lived in separate neighborhoods and went to separate schools and churches. Generally, black neighborhoods were poorer and black schools inferior. So Arthur Wright worked hard to improve life in the black community.

Marian stands in front of her mother in this photo of the Wright family. A young family friend stands to the right of Marian.

Since black children weren't allowed to play in the white people's park, he put in a playground behind his church. He wanted to build a swimming pool, but there was never enough money. The white people's swimming pool was near his home, but blacks were not allowed there. They had to swim in the creek, which was often very dirty.

Whenever an outstanding black man or woman came anywhere near Bennettsville, Arthur Wright took his children to see that person. Marian's father saw value in exposing his children to people who started out poor and became admired for their achievements. He himself never forgot how, as a young preacher, he heard the great black leader and educator, Booker T. Washington, speak. Washington believed in black people helping themselves—"pulling themselves up, getting an education, buying land, starting small businesses."

Arthur Wright died of a heart attack when Marian was fourteen. She was devastated. She missed him deeply and never forgot what he taught her about the importance of education. She studied hard in her all-black school and did well. Literature was her favorite subject, especially Rus-

Segregation meant that blacks and whites not only lived, learned, and worshipped separately, but were even entertained separately: This photo shows the entrance to a "Colored Balcony" in a movie theater.

sian novels. Her mother encouraged her to take piano and voice lessons for a possible career in music. But Marian was thinking about a career in the Foreign Service, a government organization that trains people and places them in jobs in U.S. embassies abroad.

After *graduating* from high school in 1956, Marian attended Spelman College, an all-black school in Georgia. She did very well and won an award at the end of her second year. The award enabled her to take classes and spend her third year in Europe. Marian was excited at this wonderful opportunity to live in another part of the world. Here she was, a young black girl brought up in a poor southern town, being sent to Europe, all expenses paid.

Europe was very different from the United States' segregated South. The color of her skin was not as important to people as the kind of person she was. During the school year she studied in Switzerland. She did well enough to receive another award, which allowed her to live in Russia the following summer. Marian was thrilled because she had wanted to see Russia ever since high school.

In the fall of 1959, she returned to Spelman College for her final year. She wondered how she would fit into a segregated society again. During the year she had been gone, however, the struggle against segregation and for the equality of black people had spread. The civil rights movement was organized and Marian wanted to be a part of it.

The civil rights movement, headed by such leaders as Martin Luther King, Jr., was a crusade for equal rights for all Americans. The U.S. Constitution guarantees every citizen certain rights, but for many years, these guaranteed liberties were denied to blacks and other minorities. They were not allowed to use the same hotels, parks, restaurants, and other public places as white people. Children had to attend separate schools, usually not as good as "white" schools. Many black adults could not vote to elect leaders to represent them.

In the 1960s, blacks and whites banded together to fight such unjust racial discrimination and segregation in America. Martin Luther King, Jr., believed in the power of the people gathered together to overcome unequal treatment of minorities. His weapon was nonviolent protest. That meant peacefully disobeying illegal and immoral laws. He taught his followers never to respond to violence with more violence.

Marian and her classmates had an opportunity to take a stand for civil rights in March 1960. Students from Spelman, Morehouse, and other black colleges in the Atlanta area decided to stage a sit-in at the City Hall cafeteria. (A sit-in is a nonviolent protest against segregation. Protesters sit in a segregated place to show their resistance to discrimination.) Marian and the other black students planned to sit in the white people's section of the cafeteria.

The night before the sit-in, Marian put a notice on the bulletin board of her dormitory asking volunteers to sign up. She knew they could be arrested for their protest. She called her mother and told her what she planned to do. Her mother didn't

Marian during the time she was a student at Spelman College.

Young people link arms during a civil rights demonstration in the early 1960s. As a college student Marian participated in such protests to end segregation and unfair treatment of African Americans and others.

object, so Marian packed a book to read in case she had to go to jail.

At the sit-in the next day, fourteen Spelman students, including Marian, were arrested. Instead of being embarrassed about spending the night in jail, Marian was proud that she had stood up to discrimination.

Marian also volunteered at the local office of the National Association for the Advancement of Colored People (NAACP), an organization dedicated to fighting racial discrimination. Her job was to look at all the complaints of unfair treatment that came in. She said, "I got so angry at the number of people—poor people, black people—who came to the office who needed legal help and couldn't get it." She knew this was because many white lawyers wouldn't take civil rights cases. So she decided to become a lawyer to help black people.

Wright graduated first in her class at Spelman and won a scholarship to Yale Law School. She joined a student civil rights group at Yale called the Student Nonviolent Coordinating Committee

(SNCC—pronounced *snick*). SNCC's goal was to end racial discrimination in America by peaceful means. Often this meant disobeying laws members felt to be unfair and immoral. One of the leaders of the group was Bob Moses, a former teacher.

When Moses talked about a campaign to register black Mississippians to vote, Wright listened with great interest. Very few blacks in Mississippi had ever voted. Some did not understand that they had the right to vote. Others didn't realize that voting gives people power. Wright wanted to help show blacks that electing their own leaders would give them a better life.

Completely opposed to the idea of black leaders was the Ku Klux Klan. Founded in the 1860s after the Civil War, the Klan is a group that believes white men are superior to all other people, especially blacks. During the 1960s, whenever anyone tried to help register black Americans, the Klan made threats to prevent their registration. Sometimes Klansmen beat people up. Other times they dressed in white robes, hid their faces behind white hoods, and did such things as burn crosses on

Ku Klux Klan members rally around one of their symbols, a burning cross. The Klan often threatened civil rights workers by burning crosses outside their homes.

lawns or torch houses of black activists. (An "activist" takes action for a cause.) Some Klansmen even murdered people.

In spite of the dangers from the Ku Klux Klan and others who opposed civil rights, Moses went to Mississippi in 1961 to be in charge of the voter registration campaign. He worked hard to help black people register to vote. During spring vacation of her third year in law school, Wright went to the SNCC office in Greenwood, Mississippi, to help.

On Wright's last day in Mississippi before returning to Yale, she, Moses, and several SNCC volunteers took a group of people to a courthouse to help them register to vote. The police were waiting with German shepherd dogs to scare them away. The dogs looked menacing, but Wright didn't think the police would use them against innocent people. She helped Moses and the other volunteers line everyone up in front of the courthouse door.

Suddenly the police let the dogs loose. They attacked the people in the voter registration line. One of them jumped on Moses and tore his pants. Wright couldn't believe what was happening. She hadn't brought people to court to be attacked by dogs! Fortunately, no one was killed, but several were hurt by the vicious dogs.

The police started arresting the SNCC volunteers. Wright was at the end of the line, and Moses threw her his car keys before he was led away. She drove to the SNCC office to get bail money and a lawyer who would sympathize with the volunteers' cause. Wright knew that meant a black lawyer.

Even though blacks made up almost half the state's population, there were only three black lawyers in all of Mississippi. They were in Jackson, 96 miles (154 kilometers) away. That was when Marian Wright knew she had chosen the right profession. As a lawyer, she would be able to help people who had been unjustly treated because of their race.

She finished her final year of law school, and then spent a year in New York City at the NAACP learning how to practice law to further civil rights causes in the South.

In 1964, Marian Wright headed for the heart of the civil rights struggle—she opened a law office in

Civil rights workers persisted despite threats. Here a young man registers a Mississippi woman to vote. Wright was very active in black voter registration in Mississippi.

Like Wright's fellow SNCC volunteers, this man was arrested for civil rights activism. He belonged to a group, the Freedom Riders, that traveled by bus through the South to desegregate bus stations and other places.

Jackson, Mississippi. There were still only three black lawyers practicing in the state—and they were men. Marian became the first black woman lawyer in Mississippi.

This was also the year of the Mississippi Summer Project, sometimes called Freedom Summer. Thousands of students from northern colleges came to Mississippi to help register black voters. Teachers, lawyers, ministers, and rabbis also volunteered. These activists believed strongly in the civil rights movement.

Many white Mississippians were very hostile to the civil rights workers. Shootings and bombings occurred regularly. Workers were injured and even killed. Wright always remembered to start her car with the driver's door open so that if a bomb went off she might escape. One day, three SNCC volunteers (two whites and a black) were arrested. They were held in jail until after dark. Then the sheriff turned them over to the Ku Klux Klan, who murdered the young men.

There were hundreds of other arrests, and Wright kept busy getting blacks and civil rights activists out of jail. People were often mistreated.

Wright received an award from Mademoiselle *magazine for her work during Freedom Summer. A* New York Times *editor congratulates her for her achievement in this photo.*

She recalled, "That summer, I very seldom got a client out of jail who had not been beaten, who didn't have bones broken or teeth missing."

Wright was outraged at how blacks were being treated, but she didn't allow her emotions to show. Instead she tried to think of a way to deal with the racism in Mississippi. Maybe if blacks could organize, they might overcome the injustices they suffered. Wright especially wanted to help poor children grow up to a better way of life. She believed that by helping children, we might have a more just society.

People in Washington, D.C., were also thinking about helping the poor. President Lyndon Johnson started his "War on Poverty" program in 1964. One part of this program was called "Project Head Start." Head Start is a program that prepares four-year-olds for kindergarten by educating them in preschools. Poor children learn what more well-to-do four-year-olds often learn at home or in private preschools. They are also given nutritious meals and snacks, as well as medical checkups.

Head Start centers were set up all over the nation. All a state needed to do to begin a Head

Start program was apply to the U.S. government for money to run it. But Mississippi did not apply. Most of the poor children in the state were black, and many of the white politicians who ran Mississippi did not care about helping them.

This made Wright very angry. But she was determined to bring Head Start programs to the children of Mississippi. She formed an organization of church and civil rights groups that applied to the U.S. government for funds. The organization received a grant of one and one half million dollars to set up Head Start centers throughout Mississippi. During the first year of the program, 12,000 children attended these special classes. Wright later said, "It was one of the most exciting educational programs for poor folk in the nation."

But there were many more children in the state who needed Head Start, and there were not enough programs to go around. Some children never had enough food to eat. Many parents couldn't afford to take their sick children to doctors. Poor families, black and white, needed Head Start so their children could grow strong bodies and learn enough to get a good start in school.

Children in this Washington, D.C., Head Start center learn while getting a healthy meal. Wright struggled to bring Head Start to Mississippi.

In April 1967, Senator Robert Kennedy returned to Washington from his visit to Mississippi, a visit during which he and other senators saw just how bad things were for some of the state's residents. He went to the secretary of agriculture and told him something had to be done to help these hungry people. The secretary agreed to send a group from the Department of Agriculture to Mississippi to investigate. Kennedy's young legal assistant, Peter Edelman, went with the group to make sure the members saw all the misery the senators had seen.

Peter Edelman was a white lawyer from Minneapolis, Minnesota, with a degree from Harvard Law School. The first time he met Marian Wright in Mississippi, he was impressed with her and her commitment to poor children and their well-being. The second time they met, he invited her to dinner, and they talked until midnight. The next time he came to Mississippi, they got together again and shared their feelings about hungry children. He admitted, "This time, it became clear that something was developing between us."

Peter returned to Washington, and Marian kept trying to get more money to set up additional Head Start programs in Mississippi. But money was hard to get. Wright realized that the people in Mississippi couldn't solve their problems without help from the federal government in Washington. She decided she would be more effective working for the poor if she lived in Washington, D.C. That was where the money was. That was also where Peter Edelman lived.

In March 1968, Wright moved to Washington. She received a grant from the Field Foundation to study ways to help the poor benefit from government programs. With the money she set up the Washington Research Project and began to speak out for the poor people of America.

This was a tragic time in American history. In April 1968, Martin Luther King was murdered in Memphis. In June, Robert Kennedy was shot to death in Los Angeles. Both men had been heroes to Wright, and she was devastated. America seemed to be filled with hatred.

The only bright spot in Marian Wright's life that year was her marriage to Peter Edelman on

July 14. A chaplain from Yale performed the ceremony in the backyard of a friend's home in Virginia. Marian was a black Baptist, and Peter was a white Jew. Some people didn't approve of the marriage, but Marian said, "You don't marry races. You marry individuals."

After the couple's honeymoon, Marian Wright Edelman went back to work on the Washington Research Project. She and her small staff focused on education. They were amazed to learn how little of the government money given to schools throughout the country was being spent on poor kids. They wrote a report that *The Washington Post* newspaper published on its front page.

Edelman was excited that her report had made headlines. She thought perhaps Congress or the Department of Health, Education and Welfare would finally do something to help poor children. Wright was disappointed to find that although everyone talked about the situation, no one did anything about it. She remembered, "That was my first big political lesson in Washington."

Marian and Peter just after they were married.

She learned her second lesson when the U.S. Congress decided to turn Head Start programs over to the states. Edelman had to do something to prevent this from happening. She knew Mississippi and other states that didn't want the program would get rid of Head Start. Immediately she met with a congressman who backed Head Start and told him he had to protect the program.

He asked her, "What are you for, and who are your troops?" He meant that to convince Congress to fund Head Start from Washington, Edelman needed to focus all her efforts on that one goal. More importantly, she must organize people to support it.

Edelman organized her troops. They were all people who were interested in helping poor children learn. She put together a coalition—a group of people and organizations with a common goal. It included church groups, women's organizations, and the National Education Association. The coalition wrote a proposal for a law, or bill, that would see that all states had Head Start programs and that many more preschoolers received schooling and health care.

Before a bill can become a law in the United States, it must be introduced in the Senate or House of Representatives. Members of the House and Senate study the bill and vote on it. Edelman and the coalition were thrilled when the bill passed in both the House and the Senate.

Like all bills, Edelman's then went before the president. But President Richard Nixon refused to approve the bill. He vetoed it. He said families, not the government, should be responsible for teaching preschoolers. The bill did not become law. Edelman never thought a president would veto help for children.

The lesson Edelman learned from this experience was that children had no voice in the United States government. They needed someone to look out for their interests. She decided to devote herself to speaking out for America's children, because they couldn't speak out for themselves.

In 1973 she expanded the research project into the Children's Defense Fund (CDF). The CDF focused on the needs of children all over America, especially poor children. It tried to make people understand how a child could not do well in school

The child's prayer and drawing on the cover
of the CDF publication Edelman holds here
also became the organization's logo.

if he or she was hungry or sleepy—if the family had no money for food, or if the child stayed awake half the night in a noisy homeless shelter. The CDF also tried to focus attention on abused and neglected children.

One of the CDF's first staff lawyers was a young woman named Hillary Rodham. She and Edelman met in 1969, while Rodham was a law student at Yale University, long before she married Bill Clinton, who would still later become the forty-second president of the United States. Rodham was impressed by what Edelman had to say about the needs of underprivileged children. She asked to work for the Washington Research Project during the summer. She later said, "From that experience . . . the world opened up to me, and gave me a vision of what it ought to be because of the work of people like Marian."

The two women worked well together on CDF matters. They each took on legal fights for poor people that others would not take. They fought hard and expected no public glory. Edelman worked to raise money for CDF. Rodham became chairperson of the CDF board of directors.

Despite Edelman's busy schedule, she spent as much time as possible with her family. The Edelmans had three sons, Joshua, Jonah, and Ezra. Breakfast was an important part of Edelman family life. Washington, D.C., is a town where business is often conducted at 8 A.M. breakfast meetings. But everyone knew that Edelman would not attend such meetings. "I don't have breakfast meetings," she once said. "Breakfast is when I see my kids."

Edelman was a strict mother. The boys weren't allowed to watch television during the week. Every summer they had to read a certain number of books. She told them, "If you don't pick them, I will." By reading more books, the boys could watch more television on the weekends.

The Edelman boys were brought up to be proud of their black and white heritage. They learned about both their Jewish and Baptist traditions. Each boy had a Bar Mitzvah, a coming-of-age ceremony for Jewish boys, when he turned thirteen. Twice a month, Edelman took them to the Shiloh Baptist Church, which she regularly attended. She explained, "I don't care what religion

*The Edelman family gathered for this photo at son
Jonah's 1992 graduation from Yale University.
From left are Marian, Ezra, Jonah, Peter, and Joshua.*

they choose. I just hope that they will be spiritual people."

Offering her own view of religion, she said, "I believe very much in the Gospel that says you help people who are hungry and you help people who are suffering and you help people who need help."

Edelman was raised to believe that life is about service to others, and she raised her sons with the same values. To her, "Service is the rent you pay for living, not something you do in your spare time."

Meanwhile, Edelman's work with the CDF continued. Through the 1980s, the organization grew from the small research project to an organization with a staff of over one hundred at its Washington headquarters. CDF also formed a handful of state chapters. Projects such as Child Watch were organized to make the public aware that children were in trouble. Volunteers took community leaders into homeless shelters, public housing projects, and inner-city schools so they could see for themselves how children were suffering.

Before a Child Watch visit to an inner-city kindergarten in Philadelphia, the class made a "wish list" of things they wanted for their school. On the list was a wish to visit the Please Touch Museum, a place where kids can learn by exploring museum exhibits. The school could not afford to take the children there, but one of the Child Watch visitors was director of the museum. After she visited the school with Child Watch and learned of the children's wish, she arranged for the school's kindergarten and preschool children to visit the museum free of charge. This was just one example of how Child Watch helped kids' concerns be recognized.

A CDF program for older children has to do with preventing teenage pregnancy. This was a major problem throughout the 1980s and the early 1990s. Edelman made many speeches about the problem of "children having children." Pregnant teenagers usually drop out of school, and without education, they can't get very good jobs. They and their children are usually doomed to a life of poverty. As a result of the CDF's work, some high schools (and even junior high schools) have helped students who do get pregnant to stay in school by

Children line up behind Marian Wright Edelman as she speaks at a CDF rally outside the Capitol. Their signs state some of the CDF's goals: stamping out teen pregnancy and giving kids a voice in government.

Left: Edelman took every opportunity to make the needs of children known. Here she speaks before lawmakers at a meeting on the U.S. economy. Below: Edelman welcomes President Bill Clinton to a CDF convention.

adding day-care centers in their buildings. Students could attend school while their children were cared for.

Teenagers who have turned their lives around are honored by the CDF every year. Beat the Odds Award dinners are held around the country. One winner was a girl who ran away after her mother tried to force her to join a cult. The girl put her belongings in a trash bag and left home. She sneaked into people's basements to sleep. She finally ended up in a shelter for runaways, where she received help. The girl decided the best way to change her life was to work hard in school. She got good grades, was elected president of her school's student government, and also won several school awards.

In 1992, Bill Clinton was elected president of the United States. Because of Edelman's close relationship with the Clintons, people thought the president would make her one of his close advisers or appoint her to the Supreme Court. But Edelman had no desire to be an adviser or Supreme Court justice. She pointed out, "That's not where my talents lie. That's not where my interests lie. That's not who I am." Then she added, "I was put on this earth to stay completely focused on children, and I'm going to stay 100 percent focused on children."

Marian Wright Edelman's dedication to improving the lives of America's children made an impression on many people. Senator Ted Kennedy called her the 101st senator on children's issues. She has called herself a good pest. When she doesn't get what she wants for children, she keeps hammering away. One senator told the TV program "60 Minutes" that whenever senators learn Edelman is roaming the halls of the Senate Office Building, they try to hide in the men's room. She doesn't take "no" for an answer.

In her efforts to bring the needs of America's children to public attention, Marian Wright Edelman gives speeches, grants interviews to newspapers, magazines, and TV shows, talks to clubs and political groups, and writes books and articles about the plight of children in the United States. Her message is always the same: Children are not getting a fair deal from the richest nation on Earth.

Marian Wright Edelman: the children's champion.

She has received many honors and awards for her work on behalf of America's children. In 1971, *Time* magazine listed her as one of America's two hundred young leaders. In 1990, *Ladies' Home Journal* named her one of America's most powerful women. She received a MacArthur Prize, called a "genius" award, and the Albert Schweitzer Humanitarian Award. In addition, she has been awarded more than sixty-five honorary degrees from universities and colleges.

These would be great accomplishments in anyone's life. Marian Wright Edelman appreciates that she has become the most respected voice for children in America. She says the crowning achievement in her career "would be to eliminate child poverty in America."

Chronology

1939	Born June 6 in Bennettsville, South Carolina.
1960	Graduates from Spelman College, Atlanta, Georgia.
1963	Graduates from Yale Law School.
1964–1968	Opens a law office in Mississippi and works on Head Start programs.
1968	Marries Peter Edelman on July 14.
1968–1973	Creates Washington Research Project to study how to make the laws work for poor people.
1973	Creates and becomes president of Children's Defense Fund.
1993	Celebrates the twentieth anniversary of Children's Defense Fund.

Further Reading

About Marian Wright Edelman

Marian Wright Edelman: Defender of Children's Rights
by Steve Otfinoski. Woodbridge, Conn.: Blackbirch
Press, 1992.

About Children's Rights

*Every Kid's Guide to Laws That Relate to Kids in the
Community* by Joy Berry. Chicago: Childrens Press,
1987.

About Poverty

*It's Hard Not to Worry: Stories for Children About Pov-
erty* by John M. Barrett. Cincinnati, Ohio: Friendship
Press, 1988.

Index